YOUR KNOWLEDGE HAS VALUE

Bibliographic information published by the German National Library:

The German National Library lists this publication in the National Bibliography; detailed bibliographic data are available on the Internet at http://dnb.dnb.de .

Imprint:

Copyright © 2001 GRIN Verlag, Open Publishing GmbH
Print and binding: Books on Demand GmbH, Norderstedt Germany
ISBN: 9783640866939

This book at GRIN:

http://www.grin.com/en/e-book/1774/tcp-ip-the-internet-protocol-stack

Torsten Laser

TCP/IP - The Internet Protocol Stack

GRIN Publishing

GRIN - Your knowledge has value

Since its foundation in 1998, GRIN has specialized in publishing academic texts by students, college teachers and other academics as e-book and printed book. The website www.grin.com is an ideal platform for presenting term papers, final papers, scientific essays, dissertations and specialist books.

Visit us on the internet:

http://www.grin.com/

http://www.facebook.com/grincom

http://www.twitter.com/grin_com

Fachhochschule
Hannover

TCP/IP

The Internet Protocol Stack

Torsten Laser

Technisches Englisch
SS 2001

Contents

1. Introduction

Scientists declare that the reason for human predominance in nature can be found in communication. Communication means the exchange of information. Communication enables the creation of a social order which is a condition for a peaceful coexistence of all individuals. Since technical progress has made computer communication possible, utilizability of computers seems to have multiplied. LANs (Local Area Network) link many PCs (Personal Computer). So employees of a company can share documents, information sources and different programs. WANs (Wide Area Network) connect branch offices on a continent with each other. But there is one very network, which is the most important one and which ties millions of computers anywhere in the world together: the Internet.

The Internet is a GAN (Global Area Network), which means that a computer anywhere in the world can go online (can be part of the Internet). This computer only needs a telephone connection and some rules how to communicate with all the other computers in the Internet. These rules form the TCP/IP protocol stack. Although there are many different protocol stacks for the different types of networks, TCP/IP has become the most important protocol stack of the Internet.

2. History of TCP/IP

At the end of the fifties, the Department of Defence sought a way to ensure communication between military bases and cities after a nuclear attack. But neither any cable nor any computer would be able to resist the power of nuclear bombs. And if there was a central authority, which should control the network, this authority would probably be one of the first targets to be bombed. In 1964 the scientists of the Department of Defence found that only a decentralised network could be the solution. In such a network, information is not directly transmitted from sender to recipient as known from a telephone connection. Since a network consists of many computers, the whole network can be subdivided into many knots. Each computer in this network forms such a knot. In a decentralised network, information is transmitted from knot to knot until it reaches its destination. If one knot is destroyed, there will still remain other knots to transfer the information. This transmission is called "Dynamic Rerouting".

In the sixties, this draft of a network was tested by several American universities (namely the Massachussetts Institute of Technology (MIT) and the University of California Los Angeles). In 1968, a subcompany of the Department of Defence, the Advanced Research Project Agency (ARPA), developed the first decentralised network and was in charge of it. High-speed-computers formed the knots of that network. By the end of 1969 a network came into existence, which was called the ARPANET and which consisted of four knots. One of these knots could be operated by another knot via remote-control. This means, that a user at any knot was able to control a computer which could be right at the other end of the continent. This was of high value since computer time was quite precious and expensive, these days. In 1971, this network was made up of 15 knots. In 1972, 37 knots already formed the ARPANET. Soon the system was extended to transmit files and news via e-mail (electronic mail). Only military personnel or military scientists had access to that network. But this restriction was soon given up. The first two years had shown, that the ARPANET was not mainly used for remote-control but for information exchange.

The ARPANET grew very fast, because of its decentralised architecture. Computer of any Operating System (OS), i.e. MacOS, MS-DOS, WINDOWS or UNIX were able to join this network. The computer only had to use the "Network Control Protocol" (NCP), which was later replaced by the actual standard "Transmission Control Protocol" (TCP/IP, where IP is the abbreviation for *Internet Protocol*) in 1982. In 1973, there was the first international APRANET connection to Great Britain and Norway. This connection was called "DARPA Internet" or simpler: Internet. One year later, the ARPANET consisted of 1000 knots, which were from now on called hosts because these computers are hosting the information.

Nowadays the Internet is growing faster than the telephone networks or the fax services. The diagram in figure 1 gives an idea of the growth of the Internet in the last ten years.
This survey was made by the "Internet Software Consortium" (www.isc.org).

Internet Domain Survey Host Count

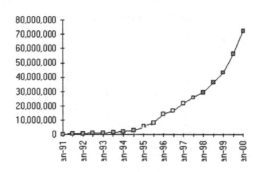

Figure 1 Internet Hosts

3. TCP/IP and the ISO 7-Layer Reference Model

The concept of a layering model is shown in figure 2. Sender and receiver can only communicate through different layers and each layer has its own interface to the neighbouring layer.

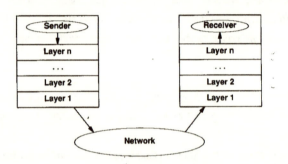

Figure 2 Conceptual organization of protocol software in layers

TCP/IP is based on the ISO 7-Layer Reference Model, which was done by the *International Organization for Standardization*. This ISO Model contains 7 conceptual layers as figure 3 shows.

Layer	Functionality
7	Application
6	Presentation
5	Session
4	Transport
3	Network
2	Data Link (Hardware Interface)
1	Physical Hardware Connection

Figure 3 ISO 7-Layer Reference Model

6

The TCP/IP-protocols did not arise from a standards commitee, but came instead from research by different universities in the U.S.A. Let us take a closer look at the two models and examine each layer.

In the **Physical Layer** all standards for physical interconnection between host computers are specified. This includes which type of cable is used, which type of plugs are used and also the electrical characteristics of voltage and current.

The **Data Link Layer** defines how data travels between a host and a packet switch. The format of frames and the way how to recognize frame boundaries are specified. The protocols of the Data Link Layer include error detection, like a checksum or a "Cyclic Redundancy Check" (CRC).

The **Network Layer** specifies the concepts of destination addressing and routing. It can also contain error detection routines, especially when a number of bits is added to the header of the data packet.

The **Transport Layer** again provides error detection routines. It gives a reliability that the protocols in the lower layers did work correct.

The **Session Layer** describes how protocol software can be organized to handle all the functionality needed by application programs. For example this layer offers the protocol for remote terminal access.

The **Presentation Layer** is intended to include functions that many application programs need when using the network. Typical examples include standard routines that compress text or convert graphics images into bit streams for transmission across a network.

The **Application Layer** includes application programs that use the network, for example electronic mail or file transfer programs.

Where is the difference between the ISO Model and the TCP/IP Model ?

The diagram in figure 4 shows, that the TCP/IP-Model contains only four conceptual layers.

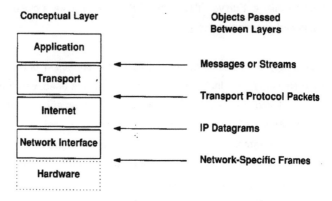

Figure 4 The TCP/IP Internet Layering Model

The **Network Interface Layer** is the lowest level. This is responsible for accepting IP datagrams and transmitting them over a specific network. The concept of transmission is defined, e.g. Ethernet, Token Ring, ATM, FDDI and so on.

The **Internet Layer** handles the communication from one machine to another. It handles incoming and outgoing datagrams, checks their validity and uses the routing algorithm to decide whether the datagram should be processed locally or forwarded.

The primary duty of the **Transport Layer** is to provide communication from one application program to another. Such communication is often called end-to-end. It regulates the flow of information, provides reliable transport and ensures that the data arrives without error and in sequence.

At the highest level, the **Application Layer**, users invoke application programs that access services available across a TCP/IP-Internet. Each application program chooses the style of transport needed, which can be either a sequence of individual messages or a continuos stream of bytes.

4. TCP/IP System Protocols

It is important to understand that:

TCP is a communication protocol, not a piece of software.

The difference between a protocol and the software that implements it is analogous to the difference between the definition of a programming language and a compiler.

There are a lot of different system protocols, which one can find in the Internet Layer and the Transport Layer. We will take a closer look at the two fundamental protocols: _TCP_ and _IP_. These are mainly used in internet communication.

IP - Internet Protocol

IP stands for: _Internet Protocol_. It is always used together with TCP. The Internet Protocol defines the "internet datagram", sometimes referred to as an "IP datagram" or merely a "datagram". The datagram is divided into header and data areas.

The datagram header contains the source and destination addresses and a type field that identifies the contents of the datagram. Figure 5 shows the general form of a datagram.

Bit-No. 0   4   8   16   19   24   31

VERS	HLEN	SERVICE TYPE	TOTAL LENGTH		
IDENTIFICATION			FLAGS	FRAGMENT OFFSET	
TIME TO LIVE		PROTOCOL	HEADER CHECKSUM		
SOURCE IP ADDRESS					
DESTINATION IP ADDRESS					
IP OPTIONS (IF ANY)				PADDING	
DATA					
...					

Figure 5 General form of an internet datagram

The header contains many details of the datagram. I would like to mention only a few. The first 4-bit field contains the version of the IP protocol that was used to create the datagram. HLEN and TOTAL LENGTH give information about the length of the header (HLEN) and the total length of the datagram.

The field TIME TO LIVE specifies how long, in seconds, the datagram is allowed to remain in the internet system. This is important because that guarantees that datagrams cannot travel around an internet forever, even if routers route datagrams in a circle.

The field HEADER CHECKSUM ensures the integrity of header values. The fields SOURCE IP ADDRESS and DESTINATION IP ADDRESS contain the 32-bit IP addresses of the datagram's sender and intended recipient.

This guarantees a connectionless, unreliable, best-effort packet delivery system.

TCP – Transmission Control Protocol

TCP stands for *Transmission Control Protocol* and is the second fundamental protocol of the Internet.

The protocol specifies the format of the data and acknowledgements that two computers exchange to achieve a reliable transfer. TCP specifies how two communicating machines recover from errors like lost datagrams. It is also specified how two computers initiate a TCP stream transfer and how they agree when it is complete.

The unit of transfer between the TCP software on two machines is called a segment. Figure 6 shows the format of a segment. Each segment is divided into two parts, a header followed by data. The header carries the expected identification and control information.

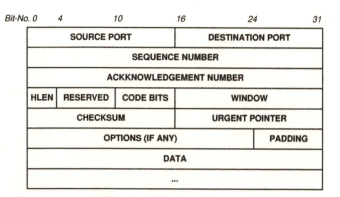

Figure 6 General form of a segment

The fields SOURCE PORT and DESTINATION PORT contain the TCP port numbers that identify the application programs. We will get to know these port numbers later in this text. The SEQUENCE NUMBER identifies the position in the sender's byte stream.

Again we find the CHECKSUM field, which contains a 16-bit integer checksum. It is used to verify the integrity of the data as well as the TCP header. The CODE BITS are used for marking urgent data, acknowledging transmission, resetting the connection and synchronizing sequence numbers.

The *Transmission Control Protocol* defines a reliable stream delivery. TCP provides a full duplex connection between two machines, allowing them to exchange large volumes of data efficiently.

TCP is very flexible, because it makes few assumptions about the underlying delivery system. It also provides flow control and allows systems of widely varying speeds to communicate.

5. TCP/IP Application Protocols

The rich functionality associated with TCP/IP results from a variety of high-level services supplied by application programs. There are a lot of application programs and I want to mention only the most important ones.

Application programs are always identified by their port numbers. These are 16-bit codes, which are found in the segments.

a) TELNET

This is a simple remote terminal protocol, which allows the user at one site to establish a TCP connection to a login server at another. *TELNET* then passes keystrokes from the user's keyboard directly to the remote computer as if they had been typed on a keyboard attached to the remote machine.

TELNET also carries output from the remote machine back to the user's screen.

TELNET is widely avaible and it accepts IP addresses. The port number of *TELNET* is 23.

b) FTP (File Transfer Protocol)

File transfer is among the most frequently used TCP/IP applications. *FTP* contains the details of authorization, naming, and representation among heterogenous machines, which make the protocol quite complex.

The users view *FTP* as an interactive system. Once invoked, the client performs the following operations repeatedly: read a line of input, interpret the command and its arguments and finally execute the command.

FTP uses whole-file copying and provides the ability for users to list directories on the remote machine as well as transfer files in either direction.

The port numbers of *FTP* are 20 and 21.

c) HTTP (Hypertext Transfer Protocol)

The *Hypertext Transfer Protocol* is known to everyone using the "World Wide Web". It provides fast and efficient transmission of information from distributed systems. It is used for transmitting hyper-media like texts, pictures, audio-data and animated data. *HTTP* is based on requests and replies. Connections are built on request, after the transmission the connections will be closed. *HTTP* uses *Uniform Resource Locators*, which are the well-known internet addresses like

http://www.fh-hannover.de

The port number of *HTTP* is 80.

d) SMTP (Simple Mail Transfer Protocol)

This protocol specifies a standard for the exchange of mail between two machines. The *SMTP* protocol focuses especially on how the underlying mail delivery system passes messages across a link from one machine to another. Communication between a client and server consists of readable ASCII text. *SMTP* is quite similar to the UNIX command "mail". The port number of *SMTP* is 25.

e) POP3 (Post Office Protocol 3)

Mail-Servers accept messages for different users and store them in so-called mailboxes. *POP3* is similar to *SMTP*, but the users have to identify themselves by their passwords. After the authorization the messages are fetched from the server and finally erased from the server's file system.

f) DNS (Domain Name Service)

The Domain Name Service is very important in the Internet. *DNS* translates the numerical addresses into alphanumerical addresses, which are memorized easily. The domain name system uses a hierarchical naming scheme known as domain names. A domain name consists of a sequence of subnames separated by a delimiter character. For example:

www.stud.fh-hannover.de

"www" is the service, "stud" is a subdomain name, "fh-hannover" is the domain name and "de" is the top-level-domain and stands for Germany. There is a large number of different top-level-domains.

Domain Name	Meaning
COM	Commercial organizations
EDU	Educational institutions
GOV	Government institutions
MIL	Military groups
NET	Major network support centers
ORG	Organizations other than those above
country code	Each country (geographic scheme)

Figure 7 The top-level Internet domains and their meanings

When you type "www.stud.fh-hannover.de" into your browser, the *Domain Name Service* will look up the numerical IP-address, which is stored in a DNS-server. The numerical IP-address for the network of the Fachhochschule is:

141.71.24.0

This address can also be written in binary notation:

10001101   01000111   00011000   00000000

Each host on a TCP/IP internet is assigned a unique 32-bit internet address that is used in all communication with that host.

14

6. The Future of TCP/IP

The version 4 of TCP/IP, which I was talking about, provides the basic communication mechanism for the global Internet. But it has remained almost unchanged since the late 1970s. Since that time processor performance and typical memory sizes have increased, the network bandwidth of the Internet backbone has risen, LAN-technologies have emerged and the number of hosts on the Internet has risen. Although IPv4 is still doing a good job, it has to be replaced soon. The main motivation for updating IP is the imminent address space exhaustion. When IP was designed, a 32-bit address space was more than sufficient. But nowadays, with the increasing number of internet hosts, especially IP needs a change.

The new version is called IPv6 and it retains many features of IPv4. But there are also some important modifications, which can be grouped into five categories:

1) Larger addresses

> The size of addresses is now 128 bits. The address space is so large that it cannot be exhausted in the foreseeable future.

2) Flexible header format

> IPv6 uses a set of optional headers.

3) Improved options

> IPv6 allows a datagram to include optional control information.

4) Support for resource allocation

> IPv6 features a new mechanism supporting applications such as real-time video that require guarantees on bandwidth and delay.

5) Provision for protocol extension

> Perhaps the most significant change in IPv6 is a move away from a protocol that fully specifies all details to a protocol that can permit additional features.

The old IPv4 addresses can be used with IPv6. So the "old technology" can work with the "new technology". At the moment most companies are stuck to the IPv4, because a change to IPv6 will be expensive. But I think it is only a question of time, when IPv6 will be first choice.

Neither the Internet nor the TCP/IP protocols are static. So the technology is stretching and evolving. IPv6 should not be discussed in detail, but with the changes that were mentioned above, IPv6 will be even more powerful and efficent than any other network protocol.

7. Bibliography

[1]   Washburn, K., and Evans, J.: *Aufbau und Betrieb eines TCP/IP-Netzes*
       Addison Wesley, Bonn 1997

[2]   Tanenbaum, A.: *Computernetzwerke*
       Prentice-Hall, München 1998

[3]   Borowka, P.: *Internetworking*
       DATACOM-Buchverlag, Bergheim 1996

[4]   RRZN-Skript: *Netzwerke – Grundlagen*
       Hannover 1999

[5]   Lindemann, U.: Vorlesungsskript *"Rechnernetze"*
       Fachhochschule Hannover 1999

[6]   Internet-Homepage "Internet Software Consortium"
       http://www.isc.org

www.ingramcontent.com/pod-product-compliance
Lightning Source LLC
LaVergne TN
LVHW042128070326
832902LV00037B/1658

The is a short introduction to the TCP/IP protocol. The TCP/IP protocol is the foundation of all internet communication. This is an overview of the technical specification and the application of TCP/IP.

www.grin.com

Document Nr. V1774
http://www.grin.com
ISBN 9783640866939

9 783640 866939